Thayer Memorial Library

P.O. Box 5 ✧ 717 Main Street ✧ Lancaster, Massachusetts 01523 ✧ (978)368-8928 ✧ Fax (978)368-8929

in the
news™

XENOPHOBIA

THE VIOLENCE OF FEAR AND HATE

Jamie Bordeau

ROSEN
PUBLISHING®

New York

Published in 2010 by The Rosen Publishing Group, Inc.
29 East 21st Street, New York, NY 10010

First Edition

Library of Congress Cataloging-in-Publication Data

Bordeau, Jamie.
Xenophobia: the violence of fear and hate / Jamie Bordeau.
    p. cm.—(In the news)
Includes bibliographical references and index.
ISBN-13: 978-1-4358-5279-2 (library binding)
ISBN-13: 978-1-4358-5564-9 (pbk)
ISBN-13: 978-1-4358-5565-6 (6 pack)
1. Xenophobia. 2. Minorities—Crimes against. 3. Racism. 4. Immigrants—
Crimes against. I. Title.
HV6250.4.E75B67 2010
305.8—dc22

2008050791

Manufactured in the United States of America

On the cover: Top right: Protesters in South Africa march against xeno-phobia after a series of riots in and around Johannesburg killed sixty people in May 2008. Top left: Asian residents flee as xenophobic violence between Asian and white youths engulfs the town of Oldham, England, in May 2001. Bottom: Immigration supporters clash with members of the anti–illegal immigration Minutemen organization during a rally in New York City in July 2006.

contents

What Is Xenophobia?

The word "xenophobia" comes to us from the Greek language. "Xeno" comes from the Greek word *xénos*, which means foreigner or stranger, and "phobia" comes from the word *phóbos*, which means fear. When you put both words together, you get the proper definition of xenophobia: an irrational fear or distrust of foreigners.

It is important not to confuse xenophobia with racism. Racism is the belief that one race is superior to another, while xenophobia is the hatred of foreigners based on fear. While racism and xenophobia sometimes go hand in hand, it is possible for people of the same race to be xenophobic toward one another. As the United Nations Educational, Scientific and Cultural Organization (UNESCO) explains on its Web site, racism is prejudice based on differences in physical characteristics, such as skin color, hair type, and facial features. Xenophobia is prejudice based on the belief

Immigrant Population as a Percentage of the Total Population

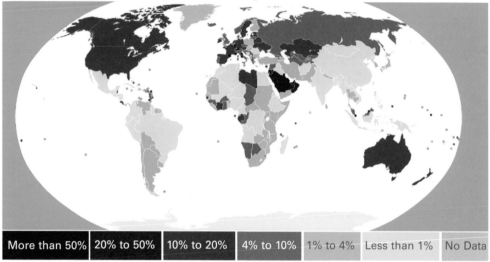

| More than 50% | 20% to 50% | 10% to 20% | 4% to 10% | 1% to 4% | Less than 1% | No Data |

This map displays the countries of the world shaded according to the proportion of immigrants within their populations. The United States has the most immigrants, with more than thirty-eight million. Immigrants make up almost 13 percent of the total U.S. population.

that certain people are outsiders and are foreign to the community or nation.

Xenophobia has been making headlines at an alarming rate, as many countries in the world experience rapid change. The population makeup and cultural identities of countries on every continent are shifting as a result of globalization and mass immigration. As these shifts are taking place, acts of xenophobic violence have been occurring all across the globe, most notably in the United States, Europe, and South Africa.

Causes of Xenophobia

There are a number of different factors that breed xeno-phobic attitudes and acts of xenophobic violence. These factors include economic distress, increased nationalism and nativism, and pressures related to immigration. In recent years, xenophobia has also grown because of global terrorism and other security threats. In a number of countries, citizens' fears about security have led to negative attitudes toward newcomers and foreigners.

Economic Strife

In times of economic strife, citizens often look for a scapegoat, or someone to blame, for their poor financial situation. When unemployment rates begin to rise, it is common for xenophobia to rise as well. Since immigrants sometimes compete with longer-term citizens for jobs, and since they are often willing to work for lower wages, they are often seen as a threat to job security.

Sylvanus Dixon, a community organizer from Sierra Leone, spoke to the BBC about the causes of xenophobia in his adopted homeland of South Africa. He claimed that jealousy and fear related to employment and income were to blame. "[South Africans] see foreigners with businesses and they don't know how they got their money," Dixon said. "That's where the jealousy is coming from. That's when the fear becomes xenophobia."

Nationalism and Nativism

Anti-immigrant sentiment sometimes leads to the rise of nationalistic political parties and nativist groups. Nationalists are people who feel a strong loyalty to their country and its traditions. In fact, nationalists may pledge loyalty to country above all else and may view their country and its traditions as more important than any other. Xenophobia and nationalism can go hand in hand, as many nationalists feel that immigrants are a threat to their countries' cultural identities. Nativists believe that native-born citizens should be afforded more rights and protections than foreign-born citizens. Nationalism and nativism often contribute to a culture of xenophobic thinking.

As immigration soars worldwide, many countries are dealing with an influx of people who speak different languages and who hold different cultural traditions and beliefs. It is common for people to be afraid of the unknown. In times of rapid change and uncertainty, many citizens resort to xenophobic views to help them justify their fears.

Xenophobia in American History

The connection between economic strife, nationalism, and xenophobia has been in place for decades. One example of this connection can be seen in the struggles of Chinese immigrants in the United States during the late 1800s. After the South seceded from the Union during the Civil War, President Abraham Lincoln passed the Pacific Railway Act of 1862 in an attempt to connect California with the rest of the Union via a transcontinental railroad. The Central Pacific Railroad Company, faced with a shortage of workers, hired Chinese immigrants to aid in the completion of the first transcontinental railroad. The work was grueling and did not pay well, but it is estimated that more than twelve thousand Chinese immigrants contributed to the project, working tirelessly to complete their sections of the railroad.

By the 1870s, however, times were tough for American workers. Chinese immigrants, who had been considered a steady source of cheap labor, were blamed for rising unemployment. Nationalist groups sprang up to protest the influx of Chinese immigrant workers. Dennis Kearney founded the California Workingmen's Party in 1874 to push a xenophobic agenda that blamed the Chinese immigrants for the problems of working Americans. Driven by the anti-immigrant sentiment of such nationalist groups, the U.S. government passed the Chinese Exclusion Act of 1882. This strict anti-immigration law barred any Chinese miners or laborers, skilled or unskilled, from entering the country for ten years. Those who broke the law were deported or imprisoned.

Above: Three Chinese laborers do railroad work.
Right: The Chinese Exclusion Act of 1882 barred
Chinese laborers from entering the United States
for ten years.

Anti-Chinese sentiment remained strong in the early
twentieth century, as shown by the passage of the
Immigration Act of 1924. Also known as the Asian
Exclusion Act, the law barred the immigration of all
Asians into the United States. The act passed because of
the widespread fear that Asian workers would take jobs
away from Americans. The law stood until 1943, when
Congress passed the Magnuson Act, allowing a limited
number of Chinese immigrants to enter the country
(about 105 people per year). In 1965, the Immigration and

Nationality Act finally removed all remaining sanctions on Asian immigrants.

One might doubt that such laws and immigration views could possibly exist today. However, the basic cycle, in which economic downturns are followed by an increase in nationalist feeling and anti-immigrant legislation, continues to this very day. Immigrants in the United States today, especially undocumented workers who have arrived illegally, have found themselves in the same position as the earlier Chinese immigrants. The country debates their rights and discusses the effects of their arrival, with xenophobic attitudes coming to the forefront on the national stage.

Terrorism, Security, and Islamophobia

The world has witnessed some spectacular terrorist attacks in recent history, with a number of them carried out by Muslim extremist groups. A troubling phenomenon that has resulted across the globe is the growth of Islamophobia, a form of xenophobia that involves prejudice against the religion of Islam and discrimination against all those who classify themselves as Muslims.

On September 11, 2001, more than three thousand people lost their lives in coordinated terrorist attacks on the World Trade Center in New York City and the Pentagon in Arlington, Virginia. The attacks were carried out by

Islamophobia is thought to be the reason why these men were removed from their U.S. Airways flight in November 2006 after praying on board.

Muslim extremists associated with terrorist leader Osama bin Laden and his organization, Al Qaeda. In the wake of this tragedy, Islamophobia skyrocketed in the United States. In fact, according to a *Washington Post*/ABC News poll published in March 2006, five years after the September 11 attacks, 46 percent of Americans said they held a "negative view of Islam" and felt that Muslims were "disproportionately prone to violence." A *USA Today*/Gallup Poll taken in 2006 found 31 percent of Americans admitting that if they were on a plane, having a Muslim man as a fellow passenger would make them feel nervous.

Following the September 11 attacks, the United States began screening airline passengers more carefully. Since the attacks, complaints against U.S. airlines about racial profiling have increased. Racial profiling is a process of singling out individuals based on their ethnic background as a means of determining if they are likely to commit a particular crime. In the case of the airlines, some Arab Americans and others have been subjected to higher scrutiny, and even removed from flights, because they look Middle Eastern. Racial profiling has been criticized as a form of xenophobia, as it encourages stereotyping, suspicion, and fear based solely on race and ethnicity.

Islamophobia is also a major issue in Europe. Islamophobia in Britain, much like Islamophobia in the United States, has been on the rise since 9/11. According to an article published in the *Times* (of London) in 2007, researchers from the European Monitoring Centre on Racism and Xenophobia found increased attacks on Muslims, including "violent assault, verbal abuse, damage to property, Muslim women being spat on and mosques firebombed." In a study done by the Pew Research Center in 2008, 23 percent of the British reported holding unfavorable views of Muslims—a striking number.

Clearly, fear of terrorism—along with economic troubles, nationalism, and concerns about immigration—has been playing a part in spreading xenophobic attitudes and viewpoints across the globe. Recently, these xenophobic attitudes have led to acts of extreme violence in several different countries. In this book, we will take a closer look at the causes and effects of xenophobia—particularly xenophobic violence—around the world, from the United States to Europe to Africa. We will look at specific examples in the news in an attempt to better understand what xenophobia is, where it comes from, and how it can be combated.

Xenophobia in the United States

At the base of the Statue of Liberty lies a poem by Emma Lazarus that symbolizes America's promise to immigrants. It reads:

Give me your tired, your poor,
Your huddled masses yearning to breathe free,
The wretched refuse of your teeming shore,
Send these, the homeless, tempest-tossed, to me:
I lift my lamp beside the golden door.

Millions of immigrants have passed through America's golden door over the past few centuries, as people from all over the world have come to the United States seeking better lives and new opportunities. America is a country of immigrants; as long as the country has existed, immigrants have helped to shape America's history and identity. As John F. Kennedy once said, "Everywhere immigrants have enriched and strengthened the fabric of American life."

IMMIGRANTS, ELL'S ISLAND   678-15

Between 1892 and 1954, more than twelve million immigrants entered the United States through Ellis Island in New York.

Yet, not all Americans are comfortable with the idea of living in a nation of immigrants. According to an NBC News/*Wall Street Journal* poll taken in June 2007, 44 percent of Americans said they believed that immigration was more harmful to the country than helpful.

The Immigration Debate

One of the major factors behind the growing anti-immigrant sentiment in the United States is the debate over illegal immigrants. Illegal immigrants are those who come to work and live in the United States without going through the legal citizenship process. They are sometimes referred to as undocumented workers, as they take jobs without having documents, or papers, proving that they are legally eligible to work and live in the United States.

Legal immigrants, on the other hand, are those who have gone through the legal process to obtain the necessary documentation for residency and employment. The legal immigration process is long and costly. In 2007, President George W. Bush raised the immigrant visa fees by more than 65 percent, a move that critics claimed would make it even more difficult for immigrants to go through the legal process. An increased emphasis on national security after the terrorist attacks of September 11, 2001, has also made the legal immigration process more difficult. The U.S. government has become increasingly selective in issuing immigrant visas to potential residents.

The challenges of the legal immigration process may account for some of the increase in illegal immigration over the past few decades. A 2005 report by the Pew Hispanic Center that was based on U.S. Census data estimated that there are as many as 11.5 million illegal immigrants living in the country, with about 700,000 new illegal immigrants entering each year between the years 1995 and 2005.

As the immigrant population rises in the United States, so does xenophobia. Nationalist groups, anti-immigrant sentiment, and brutal attacks on foreigners have appeared on the national scene in recent years, reminding the public that even in a country built by immigrants, xenophobia can still appear in extreme and violent ways.

A woman proudly raises an American flag during a 2005 naturalization ceremony in which she became an American citizen.

The Fall of the Economy and the Rise of Anti-Immigrant Sentiment

Another factor behind the rising anti-immigrant sentiment in the past decade has been the decline of the U.S. economy. According to the U.S. Board of Labor Statistics, the national unemployment rate as of November 2008 was 6.7 percent, meaning that 10.3 million Americans were without jobs.

During the presidency of George W. Bush, the United States accumulated an astonishing financial deficit. In July 2008, the White House released a report

A man protests illegal immigration at the U.S.-Mexico border in Naco, Arizona, in 2005.

estimating that Bush's financial legacy would be a national deficit of approximately $482 billion. The costs of the Iraq War, increases in spending on national security, rising crude oil prices, and cleanup costs from such disasters as Hurricane Katrina have all contributed to this deficit.

With prices soaring for American consumers in recent years, many families have been finding it difficult to make ends meet. For example, gas prices reached a record high of $4.11 per gallon in July 2008. In order to fill their gas tanks, many Americans decided to cut back on spending in other areas, causing many businesses to suffer.

Adding to the country's economic woes, a major financial crisis hit the United States in late 2008, with several financial institutions finding themselves on the brink of collapse, including Fannie Mae and Freddie Mac, two companies specializing in providing mortgages to American homeowners. When several other financial institutions collapsed, Congress passed the Emergency Economic Stabilization Act of 2008, a $700 billion bailout designed to aid failing banks in order to stabilize the economy. Though the act was passed, the economy remained in a fragile state. Between January and December 2008, about 1.9 million people lost their jobs.

The difficult economic times and rising unemployment rates in the United States have energized some anti-immigrant groups, who blame Americans' economic struggles on the growing number of undocumented workers from Mexico and Central America. Despite the various factors described above, including the costs of war and rising oil prices, anti-immigrant activists claim that it is illegal immigrants who are causing the economic downturn. They believe illegal immigrants add to the financial burden of the United States by taking money from American employers and using government services but not contributing their fair share by paying all income taxes. Anti-immigrant activists also believe that illegal immigrants are taking jobs that could be held by legal American citizens. Finally, many are concerned that illegal immigrants keep down wages for American workers because they increase the labor supply and competition for jobs.

The New Nativism: Anti-Immigrant Groups on the Rise

Frustrated by the government's failure to fully control the influx of illegal immigrants into the country, several anti-immigrant groups have sprung up along the borders of the United States. These groups are determined to stop illegal immigrants from entering their communities.

Perhaps the most well-known of these groups is the Minuteman Project. Founded in 2004 by Jim Gilchrist, a Vietnam War veteran, the Minuteman Project recruits volunteers to help protect America's borders and prevent undocumented people from entering the country. Members claim that they are simply trying to assist government border patrol agents in enforcing U.S. immigration laws. Tom Williams, head of the Minutemen in the Northwest, told the *Seattle Times* that "it's just a neighborhood watch on our border." The group also tries to call attention to the problem of illegal immigration through protests and demonstrations. On the organization's Web site, Gilchrist claims that the group's mission is to operate "within the law to support the enforcement of the law."

However, the Southern Poverty Law Center (SPLC), which tracks hate groups in the United States, posted an intelligence report in January 2005 that classified the Minuteman Project as a "nativist extremist" group, and it has published multiple reports on the hate speech and xenophobic views of the organization. According to a 2003 SPLC report, Chris Simcox, a founder of the Minuteman Civil Defense Corps, which grew out of Gilchrist's Minuteman Project, referred to Mexican and Central American immigrants as "evil people" who have no problem robbing and attacking Americans.

The rhetoric painting illegal immigrants as violent, evil criminals is echoed by several other anti-immigrant groups in the country, most notably the California Coalition for Immigration Reform (CCIR), a nationalist group founded by Barbara Coe in 1994. The Southern Poverty Law Center has listed CCIR as a hate group due largely to Coe's xenophobic statements regarding illegal immigrants. According to an article in the *American Prospect*, Coe gave a 2005 speech in which she stated that illegal immigrants were "illegal barbarians who are cutting off heads and appendages of blind, white,

In 2006, members of the Minutemen organization attempted to build a border fence in Palominas, Arizona, using barbed wire.

disabled gringos." Coe was a leading force behind the passage of Proposition 187, a measure passed in California in 1994 that barred illegal immigrants from receiving any public services, including public health care and education. Children of illegal immigrants, therefore, were denied the right to learn.

After a series of lawsuits challenging Proposition 187 were filed, the proposition was eventually ruled unconstitutional and was overturned. This defeat has not slowed the efforts of the CCIR, however. The organization continues to use fear-mongering rhetoric and an "us vs. them" mentality in its mission to reduce immigration. In the fall of 2008, the CCIR Web site invited volunteers to join them in raising awareness of the "illegal immigration nightmare" and referred to undocumented workers as "invaders" who "put the sovereignty of our country at stake" and "the future of our children at risk."

Nationalist groups claim that their anti-immigrant stances come not from a place of xenophobia or hate, but from a love of their country and a desire to secure its borders and preserve its way of life. The American Civil Liberties Union (ACLU) has been keeping an eye on nationalist groups like the Minuteman Project, defending their right to free speech while observing them to ensure that they do not abuse the civil rights of others. The ACLU has encouraged local and federal law enforcement agencies to track the groups' activities, to ensure that their actions do not break the law or include intimidation, harassment, or violence. Ray Ybarra, an ACLU Radical Justice Fellow, stated on ACLU.org, "Our concerns are based on the past history of abusive behavior by those who believe that the migrants are coming to 'destroy our way of life.' We must emphasize that these individuals are not to be dismissed as evil racists. Rather, they are symbolic of the fear and mis-understanding that exists in our society."

The Border Fence

Government construction of the border fence picked up speed after the passage of the Secure Fence Act of 2006. The barrier above is near San Luis, California.

On October 26, 2006, President George W. Bush signed the Secure Fence Act. This law enables the Department of Homeland Security to explore the possibility of building a government-sanctioned fence along the U.S.–Mexico border that would measure 700 miles (1,126 kilometers) long. If built, the fence would incorporate both virtual and physical barriers. A Rasmussen poll taken on August 17, 2007, showed that 56 percent of Americans were in favor of the border fence, but critics have expressed concerns over the xenophobic connotations of the project.

The border fence is also being criticized for potentially dividing Native American reservations along the border. Ofelia Rivas, a spokesperson for the Tohono O'odham tribe, who reside on the border of Arizona, told the *Washington Times*, "By restricting the mobility of the O'odham people, the wall prevents the free practice of their religion and their cultural traditions."

Hazleton, PA

Beyond the border fence, elected officials around the country are taking action against illegal immigrants. One of the most notable examples of this can be seen in the city of Hazleton, Pennsylvania. In July 2006, the city of Hazleton, under the leadership of Mayor Louis J. Barletta, passed the Illegal Immigration Relief Act, an ordinance designed to drive illegal immigrants out of the city. The ordinance declared that illegal immigration would lead to a lower quality of life for legal residents and blamed illegal immigrants for higher crime rates and an exhaustion of social service resources.

The Illegal Immigration Relief Act aimed to make it impossible for illegal immigrants to find residence or employment by punishing any landlord or business owner who was caught renting property to illegal immigrants or hiring undocumented workers. Under Barletta's ordinance, any landlord caught renting to an illegal immigrant would pay a fine of $1,000 per day, and any business owner caught hiring illegal immigrants would lose his or her business license for five years.

The city of Hazleton also passed a second ordinance, the Official English Ordinance, in 2006. The ordinance declared English to be the official language of Hazleton and stated that none of the city's official ordinances, policies, or decrees were to be translated from English

Community members hold a peaceful vigil at City Hall in Hazleton, Pennsylvania, in 2006 to protest Mayor Louis Barletta's ordinance.

into any other language. Civil rights groups across the country immediately denounced the two ordinances, calling Barletta's laws both xenophobic and unconstitutional. The American Civil Liberties Union of Pennsylvania, along with the national ACLU Immigrants' Rights Project and several other activist groups, filed a lawsuit against the city of Hazleton, arguing that the ordinances violated the rights of both illegal and legal immigrants in the city.

Barletta argued that illegal immigrants were the cause for the rise in crime in his community. However, the ACLU brought evidence that out of 428 violent crimes committed in Hazleton between 2001 and 2007, only four were committed by illegal immigrants. They argued that Barletta was able to pass his ordinances based not on fact, but on fear and suspicion. The ACLU also argued that in making English the official language of Hazleton, Barletta took opportunities away from legal immigrants who may not have had a full grasp of the English language. Finally, in forcing citizens to follow an English-only ordinance, the ACLU argued, Barletta violated their First Amendment rights, since all citizens are guaranteed the right to free speech under the U.S. Constitution.

On July 26, 2007, Judge James M. Munley agreed with the ACLU, declaring that Barletta's ordinances were a violation of the constitutional rights of citizens living and working in Hazleton. The ordinances were declared unconstitutional and were overturned.

Violence Toward Immigrants

A disturbing trend of anti-immigrant violence has swept the country in recent years, providing the most extreme examples of xenophobia in the United States.

A rise in violence against Latinos took center stage in a 2007 report by the Southern Poverty Law Center. Using statistics taken from the Federal Bureau of Investigation (FBI), the report shows a 35 percent rise in anti-Latino hate crimes between the years 2003 and 2006. The report lists several examples of such crimes, including the August 2007 attack against Felipe Alvarado, an immigrant working as a janitor. Alvarado was beaten by three men who screamed taunts like "Go back to Mexico" as they attacked him.

The SPLC report links the increase in anti-Latino violence to the growing media coverage of the immigration debate. The report argues that media coverage with an anti-immigrant slant, especially that of radio personalities who use the airwaves to push a hate-filled platform, is contributing to the violence toward Latinos in the United States. The report notes that xenophobic speech on the radio has the potential to incite violence in listeners, especially when the hosts promote harsh, anti-immigrant messages—for example, by characterizing immigrants from Mexico and Central America as "invaders," "criminal aliens," and "cockroaches."

The Anti-Defamation League (ADL), another organization dedicated to the protection of civil rights, filed a similar report in 2006 entitled "Extremists Declare 'Open Season' on Immigrants; Hispanics Target of Incitement and Violence." In the report, the ADL connected white supremacist groups to the rise in violence against immigrants. The report focused on the racist and xenophobic rhetoric spewed by anti-immigrant radio hosts and Web sites. The report cited Hal Turner, a radio host in New Jersey, who stated on his show on October 31, 2005: "Slowly but surely we are headed toward the solution that I have been advocating for years: Kill illegal aliens as they cross into the U.S. When the stench of rotting corpses gets bad enough, the rest will stay away."

This type of hate speech only fuels the xenophobic violence toward immigrants. The increasingly hostile rhetoric put out by various radio, television, and Internet sources promotes the idea that immigrants are evil "invaders" who deserve to be attacked. Even teenagers are being affected by this hate speech: In July 2008, five high school football players from Shenandoah, Pennsylvania, were arrested on charges ranging from third-degree murder to aggravated assault and ethnic intimidation after they beat Luis Ramirez, an immigrant from Mexico, so badly that he died of his injuries. The five teens did not know Ramirez, and it is believed that they targeted him based on his ethnicity alone. According to an article published in the *Chicago Tribune*, witnesses reported hearing the five teens shouting ethnic slurs as they punched Ramirez and kicked him in the head, knocking him unconscious and eventually causing his death.

The death of Luis Ramirez brought the issue of anti-immigrant violence back onto the national stage. In an article in the *New York Times*, Mexican American Legal Defense and Educational Fund (MALDEF) lawyer Gladys Limon said that she hoped the death of Luis Ramirez would "get attention to the wider issue that this is happening all over the country, not just to illegal immigrants, but legal, and anyone who is perceived to be Latino."

Xenophobia in Europe

3

The European Union (EU) is one of the strongest economic and political forces in the world, with close to 500 million people living in its twenty-seven member countries. The strength of the European Union has resulted in an economic boom that has drawn millions of immigrants to Europe looking for better jobs and better lives.

The influx of immigrants to EU member countries like Italy, France, and England has set off a wave of xenophobia across Europe. According to a 2007 report by the European Commission Against Racism and Intolerance, the overall picture of racism and intolerance in the European Union is "complex and worrying. Throughout Europe, these issues are giving increasing cause for political and social concern."

There are several factors fueling xenophobia in the EU. A major factor is the rise of nationalism in the face of a changing Europe. Citizens of the EU are allowed to live and work within any of the union's twenty-seven member

Muslim women protest French president Jacques Chirac's effort to ban headscarves in French schools. They are outside the French Embassy in Stockholm, Sweden, in January 2004.

countries. For some, this is an opportunity to build a better life in a fellow EU country. However, many nationalists feel that the cultural identities of their homelands are in danger. As Simon Serfaty of the Center for Strategic and International Studies told the *New York Times*, "People feel an invisible invasion; too many immigrants, the European Union, the intrusion of American culture."

This fear of a cultural "invasion" can easily be compared to the attitudes and statements of the nativist extremist groups in the United States, who claim that illegal immigrants are "invading" the country and threatening the nation's cultural identity.

The New European Nationalism

A number of political groups across Europe, most of them associated with the far right, are capitalizing on this anti-immigrant sentiment. Politicians aligned with these groups are running for office on nationalist platforms and pushing xenophobic ideas in order to win votes.

Jean Marie Le Pen, the leader of the National Front, a far-right political party in France, stunned the world by gaining enough support to reach the second round of the 2002 French presidential elections. Though he eventually lost the election to Jacques Chirac in a landslide vote, Le Pen's success as a nominee shone a light on the growing xenophobic sentiment in France. However, since 2002, Le Pen's National Front party has declined in popularity. In the 2007 presidential elections, Le Pen captured only 10 percent of the vote. Then, in February 2008, Le Pen was convicted of denying crimes against humanity and condoning war crimes after he downplayed the horrors of the Nazi occupation of France during World War II.

In Switzerland, the Swiss People's Party, an anti-immigrant, right-wing organization, is steadily rising in power and popularity. In 2003, the Swiss People's Party won 27 percent of the parliamentary vote in Switzerland. By 2007, the party claimed 29 percent of the vote, despite an anti-immigrant poster and pamphlet campaign that many labeled both racist and xenophobic. The posters, designed to promote the party's anti-immigrant stance, showed a black sheep being kicked off of

Sicherheit schaffen

This controversial poster for the Swiss People's Party is a symbol of rising nationalism in Europe.

the Swiss flag by three white sheep. Another set of posters depicted a box of Swiss passports being attacked by a mass of brown hands, with the words "Stop Mass Naturalizations" printed underneath. (Naturalization is the process of granting full citizenship to a foreign-born person.) According to the Associated Press, the Swiss People's Party also handed out pamphlets with negative statements about immigrants—for example, suggesting that many new immigrants are criminals—in an attempt to scare voters into agreeing with its policies.

In the United Kingdom, the British National Party (BNP) also promotes an anti-immigrant agenda. According to the constitution of the BNP, the party "is wholly opposed to any form of racial integration between

British and non-European peoples." Attempting to benefit from a wave of Islamophobia that swept through England following the July 7, 2005, terrorist bus bombings that killed fifty-two people, the BNP distributed pamphlets with a picture of one of the bombed buses on the cover. The words "Maybe it's time to listen to the BNP" were printed underneath. The group was widely criticized for distributing the pamphlets just before a council election in an attempt to scare up votes. In an article in the *Daily Mail*, Bob Neill, the leader of the Conservative Party, described the pamphlets as "disgraceful and sick . . . as contemptible an election tactic as I have ever seen in my life."

Perhaps the most striking example comes to us from Italy, which elected the conservative Silvio Berlusconi as prime minister for the third time in April 2008. Both Amnesty International and the European Parliament have condemned Berlusconi's government for its treatment of the Roma Gypsy population. The Roma are an ethnic group who live in poverty in camps outside of large Italian cities, including Rome and Naples. The Berlusconi government has singled them out as a source of crime. A nomadic people, the Roma are described in an Associated Press article in this way: "They often move around in search of seasonal work and live in encampments in squalid conditions with no access to health services, education, basic sanitary facilities or jobs."

Under Berlusconi's orders, the government has subjected the Roma to a widely criticized fingerprinting program, with government officials traveling to various Roma camps and demanding that the Roma submit to the fingerprinting process. According to the Associated Press, Interior Minister Roberto Maroni said the program was needed to fight crime and to identify illegal immigrants who should not be in the country. Maroni stated in the *Los Angeles Times*, "Our aim is to put an end to the disgrace of nomad camps." Yet, the European Parliament opposed this policy. The parliament passed a non-binding resolution in July 2008 that called for the end of the fingerprinting program, calling it "an act of discrimination based on race and ethnic origin."

The Roma are not the only group being targeted in Italy. The National League, a far-right political party that supports Prime Minister Berlusconi, has taken the position that all immigrants are a threat to Italian society. According to the newspaper the *Guardian*, the National League printed posters for the 2008 Italian elections that included an image of a Native American. The message on the poster said, "He let in the immigrants, and now he lives on a reservation." This political advertising was clearly designed to stir up fear toward foreigners and immigrants who are entering Italy seeking better jobs and better lives.

Xenophobic Violence in Europe

The rise of far-right political parties who thrive on anti-immigrant sentiment is an alarming sign of the growing xenophobia that is spreading across Europe. Even more disturbing are the outbreaks of xenophobic violence that have taken place in several countries throughout the continent.

Great Britain

A rise in xenophobic sentiment across Europe has led to a rash of violence against immigrants in several countries. In Britain, for example, the *Sunday Times* reported a 12 percent rise in "racially and religiously motivated attacks" between 2006 and 2007.

On May 26, 2001, a series of extremely violent riots broke out in and around the town of Oldham, South Manchester, England. Sparked by the ever-growing tensions between white and Asian members of the town, the incident, known as the Oldham Riots, lasted for three days. The term "Asian" has a slightly different meaning in Britain when used to describe one's ethnicity. The Asian community of Oldham, which constitutes 11 percent of the total population, consists mainly of citizens of Pakistani and Indian descent.

The riots involved violence on the part of both white and Asian youths. A fight at a fish and chip restaurant

Riot police attempt to stop the chaos of the Oldham Riots, which broke out between Asian and white youths in 2001.

sparked the violence, as Asian and white youths attacked each other with racial slurs. Soon after the fight, white youths were seen throwing a brick through the window of a pregnant Asian woman's home and throwing stones at Asian children. Asian men responded by throwing gasoline bombs at a local white pub. The violence only escalated from there, and gasoline bombs, stones, and broken bottles were hurled through city streets.

Tensions between whites and Asians in and around Oldham had been brewing for years prior to the Oldham Riots. A report filed by the British Home Office on the topic of "community cohesion" investigated the cause of the riots. Also known as the Cantle Report, the study blamed the riots on the long-term segregation between racial groups living in the Oldham area, with cultural misunderstanding, fear, and distrust growing between the groups as a result.

Poverty is also a major issue in Oldham. The Cantle Report suggested that the combination of racial segregation and the growth of extremism among disillusioned young people were to blame for the violence. "There is little wonder that the ignorance about each others' communities can easily grow into fear; especially where this is exploited by extremist groups determined to undermine community harmony and foster divisions," the report noted.

After the riots, local members of the community spoke out about the need to find a cultural common ground between native-born and foreign-born citizens. As Ashid Ali, head of the Oldham Bangladeshi Youth Association, told the BBC, "We need to have better understanding of each other's communities rather than living our separate lives in the same town."

Italy

Violence toward minority groups is also on the rise in Italy. In May 2008, Amnesty International released a report detailing the rise of xenophobic violence in the country. Daniela Carboni, an Amnesty International spokesperson, told *Newsweek*, "We are facing a wave of racism affecting all immigrants in Italy, including those who are documented."

A Roma Gypsy camp is set ablaze and burns to the ground on May 14, 2008.

The report was released after a series of anti-immigrant attacks swept through Rome. Nicola Tommasoli, a Romanian Jew, was beaten so badly by five members of a neo-Nazi gang that he fell into a coma and died. Neo-Nazi groups have also been held accountable for repeated acts of violence against the Roma Gypsy population, including a series of arsons that destroyed several Roma camps.

The American Anti-Defamation League, a group that fights anti-Semitism and other forms of bigotry, sent a letter to the Italian interior ministry in response to these acts of violence. The letter urged the Italian government to "publicly condemn xenophobia against Roma." However, there are no signs that anti-Roma violence has slowed down in the time since the letter was sent.

In July 2008, a series of bombs were tossed from cars into a Roma camp at Via Condoni, causing the entire camp to catch fire and burn to the ground. In August 2008, a horrific event occurred in which two Roma girls, ages thirteen and eleven, drowned at a Naples beach. After their bodies were pulled from the water, the authorities left them to lie under beach towels for three hours until an ambulance arrived to take the bodies away. The most horrifying aspect of this story is the fact that all around the girls, beachgoers continued their holiday activities, acting as if the two little girls did not even exist. The indifferent attitudes of the Italian beachgoers were viewed as a painful symbol of Italy's xenophobia; even in death, the Roma girls were ignored, pushed aside, and treated as lesser human beings. As Francesca Saudino, an Italian lawyer, told the *Guardian*, "The incident has exposed a long-held social realism in our country: that many working-class people think the Roma no better than animals, and the government is using xenophobia to win votes and popularity. People are ashamed. The deaths of these girls has come to represent something more, perhaps a battle for Italy's soul."

Spain

Spain has seen its share of xenophobic violence as well. The anti-immigrant sentiment in Spain can be attributed to recent problems with the Spanish economy.

Unemployment rates are rising, and many Spaniards view foreign-born workers as a threat to their jobs and economic security. As Sebastián Salinas, a lawyer for Acobe, an immigrant rights organization, told the *New York Times*, "People are starting to say, 'We don't need immigrants. They should return to their country.'"

Thousands of immigrants gathered in Madrid on March 18, 2001, to protest Spain's extreme immigration measures.

In February 2000, after a Moroccan immigrant was convicted of robbing and murdering a Spanish woman, hoards of Spaniards stormed a Moroccan village, attacking innocent immigrants, burning their homes, and destroying their businesses. The incident was viewed as an example of the brewing xenophobia in Spain; the Spaniards merely needed a catalyst to take their rage out on the Moroccan immigrants. Abdel Hamid Beyuki, leader of the Moroccan Workers Association, described the incident to the *New York Times*. He said, "We knew there was resentment, but we had never seen this much hatred. We are all very shaken. Some people are still hiding in the hills. A lot of us aren't sleeping at night."

In February 2002, Wilson Pacheco, an Ecuadorian immigrant, was murdered at the hands of Spanish citizens. After he attempted to enter a popular Spanish nightclub, Pacheco was beaten by the doormen and thrown into Barcelona Harbor, where he drowned. According to the *New York Times*, the Spanish newspaper *El Mundo* published an editorial condemning Pacheco's murder, pointing out the senselessness and xenophobia behind the crime. "If anyone doubts that the doormen showed a xenophobic attitude," the editorial claimed, "they will be convinced by what came next: racist insults, kicks, cruelty and absolute contempt for the victim."

Amnesty International filed a report in 2002 that accused Spain of mistreating immigrants taken into police custody. The organization investigated more than 320 cases of rape, abuse, and torture as the basis of its report. According to the *New York Times*, the report also said that immigrant children "often face abuse, deportation without regard to the law or their family situation, and a lack of protection and legal representation." Amnesty International claimed that its findings illustrated the fact that "racism and xenophobia are at least as serious a problem in Spain as elsewhere in Europe."

As Europe continues to grow and change, it will face the challenge of combating xenophobia in an increasingly diverse society.

Xenophobia in South Africa

4

South Africa is a country with a long history of political turmoil. Between 1948 and 1994, the practice of apartheid—a government-run system of racial segregation—was in place, making it illegal for blacks and whites to marry, share bathrooms, eat at the same restaurants, or go to school together. Blacks were denied many basic rights and were basically treated as foreigners in their own country. Apartheid was responsible for a great deal of violence, turmoil, and political unrest in South Africa for many years.

In the 1980s, many countries, including the United States, began to pressure the government of South Africa to end apartheid by using economic sanctions and other methods. Nelson Mandela, the former leader of the African National Congress, a black political group in South Africa, was freed from prison in 1990. He had spent twenty-seven years in prison for breaking the law as he led the fight to end apartheid. In the early 1990s, Mandela and F. W. DeKlerk, leader of the National Party, began a

Illegal immigrants from Zimbabwe climb over a barbed-wire fence and into South Africa on May 27, 2008.

series of negotiations that eventually led to the end of apartheid. Mandela and DeKlerk won a shared Nobel Peace Prize in 1993 for their efforts, and Mandela became South Africa's first democratically elected president in 1994.

Post-apartheid South Africa saw a great deal of economic improvement. Many countries that were opposed to apartheid began trading with South Africa again. In recent years, the prospect of employment and economic stability has drawn immigrants from all over Africa, most notably from Zimbabwe, where poverty, oppression, and violence have taken hold under the rule of Robert Mugabe. There are thought to be as many as three million Zimbabweans in South Africa, as well as tens of thousands of immigrants from Mozambique, Malawi, Nigeria, Congo, and Somalia. Immigrants make up roughly 10 percent of the South African population, which stands at about forty-nine million people.

Recently the post-apartheid economy boom has slowed, causing massive job losses throughout the nation.

According to the BBC, the unemployment rate in South Africa in 2008 was as high as 30 percent. These economic troubles, as well as a need to find scapegoats for South Africa's rising crime rates and housing shortages, are the major factors behind a series of anti-immigrant riots that took place in and around Johannesburg in May 2008.

The Johannesburg Riots

In the months leading up to the Johannesburg Riots, concerns about xenophobic violence in South Africa appeared more frequently in the media. In a January 2008 *Daily Nation* article about Zimbabweans taking refuge in South Africa, Kitsepile Nyathi wrote, "The burning down of shacks belonging to the refugees and even public lynchings have become a common occurrence, especially in poor neighbourhoods." Daniel Shumba of the Zimbabwe Exiles Forum warned that "violent attacks on foreigners, especially Zimbabweans and Mozambicans, are worsening each passing day."

By May 2008, the violence surged out of control. An extremely violent series of riots swept through South Africa, including Johannesburg and other cities. Rampaging rioters burned immigrant villages, destroyed immigrant businesses, and brutally attacked and killed people. Remy Kasanda, an immigrant from the Congo, experienced the xenophobic violence and attitudes

The Johannesburg Riots killed more than sixty people across South Africa.

firsthand. He told *Time* magazine, "I was at work when my friends called me to tell me that my house was on fire. On my way into town, a mob attacked me with sticks." Kasanda reported that as he arrived at the hospital for treatment after his beating, "The South African doctor told me: all you foreigners must go home."

The Aftermath of the Riots

When the riots ended, more than sixty people had lost their lives, including twenty-one South Africans who were mistaken for foreigners. More than 100,000 immigrants were left homeless. The United Nations set up refugee camps in order to accommodate those who lost their homes in the riots. The *Times* (South Africa) reported that the refugees were unhappy at the camps, calling the conditions "unlivable," with leaking roofs and a lack of fresh produce on hand. In August 2008, the South African government began closing the camps, leaving the refugees with a difficult decision: they could either return to their former towns in South Africa, where they had been threatened and attacked, or they could return to their home countries, where they would face other difficult challenges, such as poverty and oppression.

As a result of the violence, the United Nations opened an official investigation into South Africa's xenophobia crisis. The UN office in South Africa's capitol, Pretoria, was criticized for not doing enough to stop the flood of xenophobia that overwhelmed the country.

The xenophobia crisis in South Africa will likely take years to tackle, although national leaders have stepped up to condemn the rioting and the sentiment behind it. According to the BBC, Jacob Zuma, the leader of the African National Congress, condemned the attacks in a speech, saying, "We cannot allow South Africa to be famous for xenophobia."

Perhaps the most moving statement to come from the riots was made by ten-year-old Fortune, a young

Immigrants board a bus back to their home country of Mozambique in an attempt to escape the violence of the Johannesburg Riots in 2008.

boy who witnessed horrific violence in his town, including rioters shouting anti-immigrant slogans and destroying homes and property. "It was totally unfair what happened," Fortune told the BBC, "because what is South Africa without Africa? Foreigners too have blood and minds and hearts."

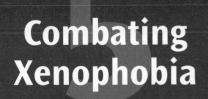

Combating Xenophobia

The world is facing a tremendous challenge in the battle against xenophobia, with xenophobic activity taking place across the globe. Yet, the world is fighting back against hatred, intolerance, and fear through education, outreach, and international discussion.

In an effort to combat the rise in global xenophobia, the United Nations held the World Conference Against Racism, Racial Discrimination, Xenophobia, and Related Intolerance in Durban, South Africa, in 2001. The conference was designed to bring global attention to the issues of racism and xenophobia. Leaders from all over the world attended in an effort to combat these issues through education and outreach. In the midst of the 2001 conference, however, the United States and Israel left "in protest over draft conference texts branding Israel as a racist and apartheid state—language that was later dropped," according to Reuters. In light of the violence that broke out in South Africa in 2008, the UN is planning a second World Conference Against Racism in 2009. The United States and Israel will both attend the rally, said Reuters, if they are guaranteed that the conference "will not become an anti-Israel event."

Also part of the UN, UNESCO developed its Integrated Strategy Against Racism and Xenophobia in 2003. UNESCO's plan includes education, scientific research, and combating racist propaganda in the media, especially in cyberspace.

In the United States, the American Jewish Committee partnered with the National Council of La Raza, a national nonprofit Hispanic civil rights organization, to head the We Can Stop the Hate campaign, a media-awareness program designed to counter the rise in hate speech that has accompanied the immigration debate in the media.

The European Union has taken its own steps toward combating xenophobia. The European Union Agency for Fundamental Rights monitors and reports on racism, xenophobia, homophobia, and Islamophobia throughout the European Union. Beate Winkler, former director of the organization, published an editorial in the *UN Chronicle* in which she described the changes needed for the EU to address its problems with racism and xenophobia. Winkler encouraged EU governments to be more inclusive, involving immigrants in the democratic process in order to promote a true multicultural society. In order to have peace, Winkler argued, the needs and voices of all citizens must be heard. "The issues of a multicultural society affect us all," she wrote, "majorities and minorities, each and every citizen."

Beate Winkler, of the European Monitoring Center on Racism and Xenophobia, said, "We need a change in attitudes."

The American Civil Liberties Union founded its Immigrants' Rights Project in 1987. The ACLU states that the project was founded "to expand and enforce the civil rights and civil liberties of non-citizens and to combat public and private discrimination against immigrants." Smaller immigrants' rights organizations, such as the Coalition for Humane Immigrant Rights in Los Angeles, work at the local level to provide community education, civil rights advocacy, and social outreach services to immigrants. Local immigrants' rights groups also seek to educate the public regarding immigration issues in an effort to combat the information that is disseminated by nativist groups.

Kids and teens are also fighting back against xenophobia, thanks to such programs as Teaching Tolerance from the Southern Poverty Law Center, which offers tools to help young people fight hate and intolerance. The Southern Poverty Law Center also sponsors the Mix It Up program, which encourages youth to break down boundaries in their own lives by doing something as simple as sitting next to someone new in the cafeteria.

Young people are getting involved in the Not In Our Town project, a community-based movement designed to combat and confront hatred, racism, and xenophobia on a local level. Not In Our Town community organizers, which include children and young adults, spread their message of tolerance and understanding through various events and town meetings.

The youth of Europe are also taking steps to combat xenophobia. Youth Against Racism in Europe is an organization devoted to fighting racism and intolerance; it has members in sixteen European countries. "Young people of all races, Asian, black, and white, must unite against racism," the organization states on its Web site. "We are the ones who have most to lose from racism and fascism, and most to gain from their defeat. United we can win."

The actions being taken by the United Nations, the European Union, and the United States—as well as the

The We Can Stop the Hate campaign (http://www.wecanstopthehate.org) is a media-awareness program that seeks to eliminate the hate speech associated with immigration.

actions taken by adults and youth within their own communities—are all positive steps toward reducing the fear of immigrants and foreigners that has led to so much violence and unrest in recent years. It is only through education, understanding, and open-mindedness that we can hope to combat xenophobic views and violence. As Beate Winkler stated in the *UN Chronicle*, "We need a change in attitudes, from a climate of fear to a climate of hope."

Glossary

apartheid A legal form of racial discrimination through government-sanctioned segregation.

illegal immigration Immigration to a country without proper consent from its government.

immigration Moving to a new country permanently.

Islamophobia An irrational fear or distrust of Muslims.

nationalist One who pledges loyalty to country above all else, and who views his or her country and its traditions as more important than any other.

nativist One who believes that natural-born citizens should be afforded more rights than the foreign-born.

naturalization The process through which an immigrant is given citizenship in a new country.

propaganda Information spread to further one's cause.

racial profiling Singling out individuals based on their ethnic background as a means to determine if they would be more likely to commit a particular crime.

racism The belief that one race is superior to another.

rhetoric A verbal or written communication.

scapegoat An individual or a group that is unfairly blamed for the problems of others.

undocumented workers Laborers who work without providing legal proof of citizenship or residency.

xenophobia A fear or distrust of foreigners or strangers.

For More Information

American Civil Liberties Union

National Headquarters

125 Broad Street, 18th Floor

New York, NY 10004

Web site: http://www.aclu.org

The American Civil Liberties Union is a nonprofit organization dedicated to the protection of civil rights through communications and legal efforts. Information on high-profile court cases involving civil rights, such as the Hazelton, Pennsylvania, case, can be found on the ACLU's Web site.

National Anti-Racism Council of Canada

#122–215 Spadina Avenue

Toronto, ON M5T 2C7

Canada

(416) 979-3909

Web site: http://www.narcc.ca//index.html

The National Anti-Racism Council of Canada is a national organization dedicated to addressing the issues of racism and intolerance throughout Canada. This organization provides information on antiracism campaigns and community-based projects throughout Canada.

Not In Our Town

c/o The Working Group

P.O. Box 70232
Oakland CA 94612-0232
(510) 268-9675
Web site: http://www.pbs.org/niot/index.html
Not In Our Town is a national project dedicated to reducing racism, intolerance, and xenophobia on a local level. Teens and their families are encouraged to get involved by creating Not In Our Town projects in their own communities. Information on how to get started can be found on its Web site.

Southern Poverty Law Center

400 Washington Avenue
Montgomery, AL 36104
Web site: http://www.splcenter.org
The Southern Poverty Law Center is a nonprofit organization devoted to tolerance education and hate-group awareness. The SPLC is a good resource for those interested in learning more about xenophobic nativist and nationalist groups.

Web sites

Due to the changing nature of Internet links, Rosen Publishing has developed an online list of Web sites related to the subject of this book. This site is updated regularly. Please use this link to access the list:

http://www.rosenlinks.com/itn/xeno

For Further Reading

Allport, Alan. *Immigration Policy*. New York, NY: Chelsea House, 2004.

Bedhad, Ali. *A Forgetful Nation: On Immigration and Cultural Identity in the United States*. Durham, NC: Duke University Press, 2005.

Gallo, Donald R. *First Crossing: Stories About Teen Immigrants*. Cambridge, MA: Candlewick Press, 2004.

Haerens, Margaret, ed. *Illegal Immigration*. Farmington Hills, MI: Greenhaven Press, 2006.

Hunter, Miranda. *Latino Americans and Immigration Laws: Crossing the Border*. Broomall, PA: Mason Crest, 2005.

Nyamnjoh, Francis B. *Insiders and Outsiders: Citizenship and Xenophobia in Contemporary Southern Africa*. London, England: Zed Books, 2006.

Ouellette, Jeannine. *A Day Without Immigrants: Rallying Behind America's Newcomers*. Mankato, MN: Compass Point Books, 2008.

Streissguth, Tom. *Welcome to America? A Pro/Con Debate Over Immigration*. Berkeley Heights, NJ: Enslow, 2008.

Tan, Shaun. *The Arrival*. New York, NY: Arthur A. Levine, 2007.

Taras, Ray. *Europe Old and New: Transnationalism, Belonging, Xenophobia*. Lanham, MD: Rowman & Littlefield, 2008.

Bibliography

ABC News Web site. "'Islamophobia' Felt 5 Years After 9/11." September 9, 2006. Retrieved August 2008.

American Civil Liberties Union Web site. "ACLU of Arizona to Provide Legal Observers During Controversial 'Minuteman' Border Watch Program." March 30, 2005. Retrieved August 2008.

Ames, Paul. "EU Warns Italy over Gypsy Fingerprinting." *USA Today* Web site, July 10, 2008. Retrieved July 2008.

BBC News Web site. "Communities Urge Action on Riot Reports." December 11, 2001. Retrieved July 2008.

BBC News Web site. "Thousands Flee S Africa Attacks." May 19, 2008. Retrieved July 2008.

British Home Office. "Community Cohesion." 2001. Retrieved August 2008 (http://image.guardian.co.uk/sys-files/Guardian/documents/2001/12/11/communitycohesionreport.pdf).

British National Party Web site. "Constitution of the British National Party: Eighth Edition." November 2004. Retrieved August 2008.

Cracknell, David. "Racist Attacks up 12 Per Cent in a Year." *Sunday Times* Web site, October 28, 2007. Retrieved August 2008.

Daily Mail Web site. "'Sick' BNP Produce Bus Blast Leaflet." July 12, 2005. Retrieved August 2008.

Daly, Emma. "Amnesty Accuses Spain of Racism." *New York Times* Web site, April 19, 2002. Retrieved July 2008.

Daly, Emma. "Brutal Death of Immigrant Shakes Faith of Spaniards." *New York Times* Web site, February 13, 2002. Retrieved July 2008.

Deane, Claudia, and Darryl Fears. "Negative Perception of Islam Increasing." *Washington Post* Web site, March 9, 2006. Retrieved July 2008.

De la Baume, Maia. "Le Pen Guilty in Defending Nazis." *New York Times* Web site, February 9, 2008. Retrieved August 2008.

DeParle, Jason. "Spain, Like U.S., Grapples with Immigration." *New York Times* Web site, June 10, 2008. Retrieved July 2008.

Elias, Marilyn. "USA's Muslims Under a Cloud." *USA Today* Web site, August 10, 2006. Retrieved August 2008.

Erlanger, Steven. "Europe's Identity Crisis." *New York Times* Web site, May 5, 2002. Retrieved July 2008.

Hawley, Caroline. "Children Terrified by SA Xenophobia." BBC News Web site, June 24, 2008. Retrieved July 2008.

Jolly, Joanna. "Migrants Tell of Township Tensions." BBC News Web site, May 15, 2008. Retrieved July 2008.

Jones, Tobias. "The Triumph of the Right?" *Guardian* Web site, May 2, 2008. Retrieved July 2008.

Kamaldien, Yazeed. "Refugees Say They Feel Unsafe." *The Times* (South Africa) Web site, July 14, 2008. Retrieved August 2008.

Kennedy, Dominic. "Asian Knife Killings Double." *The Times* Web site, April 26, 2007. Retrieved July 2008.

McDougall, Dan. "Why Do the Italians Hate Us?" *Guardian* Web site, August 17, 2008. Retrieved August 2008.

Moser, Bob. "Open Season." Southern Poverty Law Center Web site, Spring 2003. Retrieved July 2008.

Nadeau, Barbie. "Italy's Unwanted." *Newsweek* Web site, May 28, 2008. Retrieved July 2008.

Nyathi, Kitsepile. "Citizens Face Xenophobia." *Daily Nation* (Nairobi) Web site, January 28, 2008. Retrieved July 2008.

Olivo, Antonio. "Immigrant's Death Splits Blue-Collar Town." *Chicago Tribune* Web site, August 12, 2008. Retrieved August 2008.

Passel, Jeffery S. "Estimates of the Size and Characteristics of the Undocumented Population." Pew Hispanic Center Web site, March 2005. Retrieved August 2008.

Perry, Alex. "Johannesburg Is Burning." *Time* Web site, May 21, 2008. Retrieved August 2008.

Powell, Michael, and Michelle Garcia. "PA City Puts Illegal Immigrants on Notice." *Washington Post* Web site, August 22, 2006. Retrieved August 2008.

Preston, Julia. "City's Immigration Restrictions Go on Trial." *New York Times* Web site, March 13, 2007. Retrieved August 2008.

Savage. David G. "The Nation—Judge Rejects Hazleton Law on Immigrants." *Los Angeles Times* Web site, July 27, 2007. Retrieved July 2008.

Seper, Jerry. "Southwest Tribe Calls for End of Border Fence Construction." *Washington Times* Web site, July 11, 2008. Retrieved July 2008.

Simons, Marilese. "Resenting African Workers, Spaniards Attack." *New York Times* Web site, February 12, 2000. Retrieved July 2008.

Southern Poverty Law Center Web site. "Blood on the Border." Spring 2001. Retrieved August 2008.

Turnbull, Lornet. "Minutemen Watch U.S.-Canada Border." *Seattle Times* Web site, October 4, 2005. Retrieved July 2008.

UNESCO Web site. "Fight Against Racism, Discrimination, and Xenophobia." Retrieved August 2008.

Wall Street Journal Web site. NBC News/*Wall Street Journal* Poll, June 2007. Retrieved August 2008.

Ward, David. "This Has Been Building Up for Years." *Guardian* Web site, May 28, 2001. Retrieved August 2008.

We Can Stop the Hate Web site. "AJC Appeals to Cable TV Executives to End Airing of Anti-Immigrant Hate." February 15, 2008. Retrieved August 2008.

Wilkinson, Tracy. "Italy Criticized for Fingerprinting Gypsies." *Los Angeles Times* Web site, July 11, 2008. Retrieved July 2008.

Winkler, Beate. "Looking Forward to the Future: Europe's Societies Are Undergoing Change." *UN Chronicle*, Vol. 44, No. 3, September 2007, pp. 32–35.

Index

About the Author

Jamie Bordeau is a writer and librarian who devotes much of her time to working with elementary and middle school students through creative workshops and educational programming. She holds a master's degree from New York University.

Photo Credits

Cover (top left) Odd Andersen/AFP/Getty Images; cover (top right), pp. 44, 48 John Moore/Getty Images; cover (bottom) Chris Hondros/Getty Images; pp. 4, 9 Courtesy California State Railroad Museum; p. 5 Wikimedia Commons; p. 9 (inset) National Archives and Records Administration; p. 11 krtphotoslive/Newscom; pp. 14, 24 David McNew/Getty Images; p. 15 Library of Congress Prints and Photographs Division; p. 17 © Shannon Stapleton/Reuters/Corbis; p. 18 © Saul Loeb/epa/Corbis; p. 22 © David Kadlubowski/Corbis; p. 26 © Kristen Mullen/The Citizens' Voice/AP Images; pp. 30, 37 © M.E.N./Corbis/Sygma; p. 31 Bertil Ericson/AFP/Getty Images; p. 33 Ralph Orlowski/Getty Images; p. 39 Francesco Pischetola/AFP/Getty Images; p. 41 © Reuters/Corbis; pp. 43, 46 © AP Images; p. 51 Gerard Cerles/AFP/Getty Images.

Designer: Tom Forget; Editor: Andrea Sclarow
Photo Researcher: Cindy Reiman